BLESS THIS MESS

PRACTICAL PRAYERS *for*
BROKEN TOASTERS, NOSY NEIGHBORS,
MISSING SOCKS *and* OTHER
DAILY EXASPERATIONS

~ Jay Steele & Brett Bayne ~

WORKMAN PUBLISHING
NEW YORK

Library of Congress Cataloging-in-Publication Data
Steele, Jay.
Bless this mess: practical prayers for broken toasters,
nosy neighbors, missing socks and other daily exasperations/
by Jay Steele and Brett Bayne.
p. cm.
ISBN 0-7611-0398-8 (pbk.)
1. Prayers. 2. Wit and humor. I. Bayne, Brett. II. Title.
BL560.S74 1997   97-38006
818'.5407—dc21   CIP

Cover and interior illustrations by Oscar Senn

Workman books are available at special discounts when purchased
in bulk for premiums and sales promotions as well as
for fund-raising or educational use. Special editions or book
excerpts can also be created to specification. For details, contact the
Special Sales Director at the address below.

Workman Publishing Company
708 Broadway
New York, NY 10003-9555

Manufactured in the United States of America

First printing November 1997
10 9 8 7 6 5 4 3 2 1

Lord,
Please break the laws of the universe
For my convenience.
　　　　　　　—Emo Philips

The world has become a complicated and vexing place. Gone is the time when coveting your neighbor's donkey was the biggest moral challenge you had to face. It's more difficult to navigate a path nowadays in a world full of talking computers, two-career families and Coke machines that refuse to accept your last dollar bill when you don't have any change.

Sure, you can find spiritual guidance for the big issues, but whom do you call upon when your dinner's interrupted by someone selling a long-distance plan, when your computer crashes, or when the guy in front of you in the supermarket express lane has more than 10 items? You won't find these situations covered in any traditional religious texts. So that's why we decided to write this book.

It is said that God hears all our prayers. Well, now you have a collection of petitions, blessings and meditations that address the small but pressing problems of modern life. Give them a try. Have faith. As a wise man once said, "It couldn't hurt."

EARTHLY
TOILS

≈

O satisfy us with thy mercy
That we may rejoice
And be glad for all our days,
Even Mondays.

≈

EMPLOYEE'S CONFESSION

O grant me your forgiveness for
My little office sins,
Like adding extra hours when
I fill my time card in.
Forsooth, some calls are personal
I make on office phones,
And I admit last month I took
A brand new stapler home.
And then there was last Friday,
When my attitude was slack,
And I departed early,
Right behind the boss's back.
Forgive me that expense report
I padded just a bit,
With meals uneaten, phony tolls—
All this I must admit.
I know that I'll look back someday,
When I'm at last retired,
And thank you, Lord, for keeping me
From getting fired.

SUPPLICATION AT THE COPY MACHINE

Great Master of Replication,
When I feed this document into the copier,
Keep it free of paper jams and misfeeds,
Let me not see the "Add Toner" message,
Nor the "Call Key Operator" prompt.
May my copies not be collated in reverse,
Nor inexplicably reduced to 77%,
Nor stapled in the wrong corner.
And when I have an urgent job—
        just one copy—
Let me not find That Woman from
        Accounting* there
Doing 65 copies of her 40-page
        double-sided report.
Amen.

*You know, the one who takes a 20-minute cigarette break
 every day at 4:30.

MEETING
MEDITATION

Meetings, meetings every day,
Another morning's gone.
We've closed this subject twice before
And still the boss drones on.

O help these people be concise
And on the subject keep—
My eyes are glazing over and
My leg has gone to sleep.

I've tried to lead a good life, Lord—
This torture's undeserved.
So please restrict my meetings to
The ones where lunch is served.

AMBITION

O bring me the opportunity
To fulfill my potential
And live out my career dreams,
But without having to call for the
information
That Sally Struthers spoke about.

JOB SEEKER'S PETITION

God, guide me through this interview
And keep my spirits high—
Becalm my swiftly beating heart
And let my palms stay dry.

To give them the impression that
I'm poised and quite astute—
Don't let me fuss and fidget with
This itchy woolen suit.

Please let the boss be kind and fair
A trusting soul, forsooth,
Who'll not pick through my résumé
And find I've stretched the truth.

PRAYER
OF THE
COMMUTER

As I do battle on these twisting and
  dangerous byways,
Hear my plea, O Lord:
Be banished all
Ye who move into my lane without signaling!
Speed thee into darkness,
Ye who drive with your brights on!
Abandon all hope,
Ye who talk on cellular phones
And pay not attention to the road!
Get thee behind me,
  Thou '87 Nova
  Doing 45 in the fast lane!

PC PLEA

Resolve my sad computer woes—
I booted up. My cursor froze!

I pressed "Escape," I hit "Delete,"
Read IBM's instruction sheet

To no avail. It's just no use,
Without your help, I'll need a noose.

Please help me as I further strive
To fix my Windows 95.

Pray give me strength and courage when
My hard drive crashes once again.

18.9%
ABSOLUTION

Soothe those unhappy souls
At Visa and MasterCard
Who get so very righteous
When I exceed my credit limit,
Or miss one measly payment.

Let them instead understand
That money is the root of all evil.

And forgive me my overcharges
As I forgive those
Who charge dinner
And then expect me to pay
    my share in cash.

ON ADDRESSING THE MULTITUDES

Their eyes are all upon me, Lord,
　　so help me to succeed.
My fear of public speaking must
　　not keep me from this deed.
Don't let me talk too fast and leave
　　the slower folks confused—
Yea, may they pay attention and be suitably amused.
O let my voice be clear and strong and
　　not begin to choke,
And please be sure they laugh along when
　　I attempt a joke.
O don't permit the microphone to crackle or to fail,
Nor let my trembling hands and arms
　　betray my nerves and flail.
So as I use my winning smile
　　to help me through this speech,
Please let me not discover there was spinach
　　on my teeth.

WORDS TO LIVE BY

Thou gave us the Word, O Lord,
So when I take pen in hand,
Enlighten me in the ways of correct
     punctuation?
Improve my speling skills
And eliminate all unecesary typos.
Save me from my habit of using hyperbole,
Which I do a billion times every day.
Help me to stop being so redundant,
And help me to stop being so redundant.
Teach me how to properly use analogies
(Because I'm as dumb as a thirsty aardvark).
Let my vocabulary be simple and intelligible,
Unlike those rapscallions who pontificate
     vaingloriously.
Grant me the talent to write eloquently,
Because my run-on sentences,
Which I can never seem to stop doing.
And above all,
Give me the wisdom to finish what I

TEMPLE
OF
THE BODY

~

Avert all eyes from me, O Lord.
Let my supply of hats
be my shield
Until this bad haircut grows out.

~

DENTAL CONTRITION

All that I ought to have flossed
        and have not flossed,
All that I ought to have brushed
        and have not brushed:
For these I am truly repentant, Lord,
As the sound of the dentist's drill
Cuts through me like a chill wind.

Steady his hand, O Heavenly Father,
And hasten whatever he's doing to
        that rear molar.

O may he command me to rinse soon,
For the Novocain shots I received earlier
Are wearing off fast.

May it not be a crown I will require,
But only a small filling.
And whatever the need, Lord,
Please allow my dental plan to cover it.

AFFIRMATION
OF THE
NEARSIGHTED

O Master of Saline Solution,
Help place this contact lens in my eye,
Which I can barely make out in
        this steamy bathroom mirror.
If thou see fit to let it fall into the sink,
Lead me to its invisible presence
As it lays hidden among beads of soapy water.
Pray, let the residue of the cleaning solution
        not sting.
And if I am successful in adhering these lenses
        to my eyes,
Please make sure I have not switched
        left and right.
Amen.

GRACE FOR MATURITY

O Lord, thou hast provided me
This earthly body that you see.
So as my parts begin to sag
And aches and pains upon me nag,
Let me accept with willing grace
The wrinkles spreading o'er my face,
The eyesight that begins to fade,
And hair that's growing thin and grayed.
My memory, though never strong,
Gets dimmer as I go along.
Please grant me patience through it all,
        Or, better yet—an overhaul.*

*This prayer can also be found in any large-type version of the Book of Genesis.

ON
VANITY

Let my prayer come before thee,
Into thine ears hear my cry:
For my pierced tongue*
Still really hurts
A lot.

*May also be invoked for nose jobs, pierced ears,
liposuction, tummy tucks and all varieties
of minor plastic surgery.*

DIETER'S OFFERING

I lay my sufferings at your feet,
Eternally Fit Creator:
All those breakfasts of half grapefruit,
Salads deprived of dressing for lunch,
Chicken breast and steamed vegetables
        for dinner.

I have endured them all,
The fat-free,
The lo-cal,
The lite.

Unburden me, then, of those
        extra 15 pounds
Before the first weekend of summer,
So that I may appear on the beach
In the daylight.

EULOGY FOR FALLEN FRIENDS

They once grew thick and wavy, Lord,
Upon my lowly head.

Yet now that lustrous crop of hairs
Is sadly gone and dead.

I've tried the lotions, gels and sprays
Yet they're of little use.

I wear bandannas every day
And still I get abuse.

I do not ask you for myself
To ease this earthly trial

But please help all who share my plight:
   Bring baldness into style!

RELATIONS
AND
RELATIONSHIPS

~

Teach me thy way, O Lord,
And bestow your eloquence
When my four-year-old asks
Where babies come from.

~

SUPPLICATION FOR A BLIND DATE

O let him be a kindred soul, this guy
    I'll meet tonight,
A man who's kind and sensitive, who'll really
    treat me right.
He need not be a rich man, Lord,
    just gainfully employed
And comfortable discussing books and films
    that he's enjoyed.
O let him be romantic and his sense of humor keen,
A man who'll listen to my words and know just
    what I mean.
Please let his many interests span a fascinating range,
His grasp of world events not just be
    who won last night's game.
I'll try to take it slow this time, not let
    my feelings flip,
But if he's right, then please grant me
    a real relationship.

PLEA OF
ONE WHO
LOST COUNT

The miracle of life
Is truly one of thy greatest gifts,
O Lord.
But please let my lateness this month
Be just a little lateness
And not one of thy miracles.
Amen.

PARENTAL
BEDTIME
PRAYER

Now I lay me down to sleep
In hopes the baby quiet will keep.
Wake me not till there is light
And let this kid sleep through the night.

But if the crying starts at three
And my dear child won't quiet be,
Please make my spouse from bed adjourn—
Thinking that it's not my turn!

IN
CELEBRATION

Give me the strength
To survive my child's birthday party
At Chuck E. Cheese's.
Stand by me as I break up the fights,
Wipe up the spills,
And round up the stragglers.
Help the nervous, child-hating waiter
Understand the sound of fifteen kids
All shouting out their requests
At the same time.
Woe to the parents who did not think
To bring quarters,
So that their offspring might partake
Of the video-game machines.
Yet as stressful as this is, Lord,
I thank thee that at least they've
        outgrown Barney.

ON YOUNG ADULTHOOD

'Tis a gift to be living, tis a gift to be grown
But while I am staying in my parents' home
Pray help me to endure all their doting
    and fuss
Their reminders and warnings and lectures
    and such.
I know when it's cold I should wear
    a warm coat
And when I'm out late I should leave them
    a note.
I know the kitchen must stay neat and clean—
O let them realize, Lord, I'm no longer
    thirteen!*

*A counterpoint view appears in Matthew:
 "O protect me, Lord, from the folly I have done,
 For I have loaned the car keys
 To my sixteen-year-old son."

WEDDING DAY PLEA

Here I stand, O Lord, about
To utter those two words devout.
Grant me strength to say them true
And not to stammer through "I do."

It's truly been a long ordeal:
The flowers, guest list, dress and meal
Have each been subjects of debate
But somehow wound up looking great.

Help me through just one more trial
As I walk back down that aisle:
Let me have my wedding thrill
And, for today, forget the bill.

HOME IMPROVEMENT

Bless him, Lord,
For he really does try
To make himself useful
In so many ways.
If something should break,
He jumps in with a smile
With his hammers and ladders
And lubricant sprays.
But the leaks keep on leaking,
The blender's still ill.
And what started out broken
Is often destroyed.
Please help him to learn
That he hasn't the skill:
That as a repairman
He'd be unemployed.

INTERCESSION FOR THE NEWLY DIVORCED

O Heavenly Father,
Let there be a special place in Heaven
For all lawyers.

And if you want to take them there
right now
That would be OK.

INTERACTIVE PRAYER

Lord,
Please help
A) Her
B) Him
Understand that
A) A man has needs
B) "No" means no
And that I have no intention of
A) Getting married
B) Having sex
Unless we:
A) Have sex.
B) Get married.

OF
HEARTH
AND HOME

~

Who shall ascend to the hill
of the Lord?
And who shall turn off
that car alarm
That ringeth at 3:30 A.M.?

~

BLESS THIS MESS

Burnt-out lightbulbs in the bathroom,
Broken buzzer on the door,
Moldy pizza in the icebox,
Dirty laundry on the floor,
Garbage piled up, overflowing,
Cobwebs on the chandelier,
A sink full of dirty dishes—
Help us make them disappear!

We know we're not neat:
    This we confess,
But how it got this bad is anyone's guess.
With all of this clutter, we're starting
    to stress.
So we beg you, Lord: Bless this mess.

INTERCESSION
FOR
RELOCATION

Soothe my aching back
Which is weary from lifting 1100 boxes
Up four flights of stairs.
Help me to locate a good dry cleaner,
A Chinese takeout
And a video store
In my new neighborhood.
Shield me, O Lord, from the angry
        second-notice letters
That come because my creditors have not
        observed
The change-of-address forms
I so diligently filled out.
And grant me the foresight to
        think twice
Before I decide to move again.

REFLECTION ON SHARING A BATHROOM
I

O Merciful Deity
Grantor of wisdom and justice,
Please give him the presence of mind
To put the toilet seat back down!*

*This prayer is best addressed to St. Jude,
who specializes in lost causes.*

REFLECTION ON SHARING A BATHROOM II

O Lord,
Forgive me for taking thy name in vain—
But she has availed herself
Of my razor
And used it to shave her legs!*

*Compare Isaiah's protestation:
"O plague on her, Lord, for she has left her wet panty hose
hanging on the shower rod again!"

THY WILL BE REDONE

Lord, see me through this redecorating:
Where there is brown shag carpet, grant me
    a tile floor;
Where there is peeling paint, fresh wallpaper;
Where there is a shabby recliner,
    a nice leather sofa.

May the contractor not delay completion
For yet another two weeks,
Nor exceed the price estimate any further.
O grant me peace through the dust
And noise
And clutter,
That my living room may be born again!

A HYMN OF HOUSEHOLD PESTS

All things bright and beautiful,
All creatures great and small,
You've given us some little things
That need not be at all.
For instance, why the termite, Lord,
And why so many flies?
You could've skipped the cockroach, too,
If thou hadst been more wise.
The wasps, the mosquitoes and the snakes
I think were a mistake,
And spiders top the list of beasts
I wish you would un-make.
Create more things like butterflies
And ladybugs and snails,
Disposing of all creepy things
With claws and fangs and scales.
For if you won't eliminate
These pests that you have made,
I'll have to see to it myself,
Armed with a can of Raid.

LAUNDRY DAY HOMILY

If cleanliness is next to godliness, then
　　banish this mustard stain
　　from my brand-new blouse.

Let there not be a wayward Kleenex
　　in one of these trouser pockets,
　　nor a single maroon sock hiding
　　among the whites.

Because I really can't face wearing
　　pink underwear again
For the next two weeks.

PET PEEVES

Almighty Creator of Creatures,
Housebroken and otherwise—
We would truly rejoice
If our beloved cat learned to keep dead
    rodents outdoors
And not kick the contents of
    her litter box
Under the water heater.

And our beloved dog
Would be even more lovable without
    those fleas
And wood ticks.
Yea, bestow upon this aging hound
A pair of stronger kidneys—
Or else, grant our family new
    wall-to-wall carpeting.

LEASEHOLDER'S LAMENT

From the miserly landlord
 who raises the rent;
From the faucet that drips but
 they never will fix;
From the slovenly super
 who's so malcontent;
From the baby upstairs who starts
 crying at six;
From the sullen young neighbor
 who blasts his CDs;
From this lousy apartment—
 DELIVER ME!

PRAYER AT THE FRIGIDAIRE

Now I take sponge in hand
And don these trusty rubber gloves
In preparation to tackle the problem
I have avoided far too long.

O give me the courage, Lord,
To face that Thing in the Tupperware
Deep in the back of the refrigerator.
Bestow upon me the wisdom
To throw the whole thing out
Without opening the container,
For I know not what science project
Lurks inside.

PETITION
FOR A
HEADACHE

Thou who grantest
Sight to the blind
Food to the hungry
And peace to the soul
Please grant silence
To my neighbor's dog.

CURSE OF
THE
HOMEBOUND

A plague on you,
Liars and hypocrites!

Plumbers, delivery men and cable-TV guys
Who would decree that I should
stay home
Between the hours of 9 A.M. and 6 P.M.

And then not show up!*

*See the Book of Job:
"And the Lord unleashed a pestilence of locusts upon
the Land, whereupon Job was forced to sit at home all day
waiting for the exterminator."

49

WHAT MAN HATH WROUGHT

~

Oh, strange rattling noise
Deep inside my car engine—
Heal thyself!

~

AT THE ATM

Please guide those souls ahead of me
    toward the buttons that they need.

Pray grant them brains to know their PIN
    and enter their transactions in.

Yea hasten them, they're moving slow
    and yet it's not so hard, I know:
The buttons all are clearly marked.

Please help them, Lord,
I'm double-parked.

PETITION FOR THE PALATE

From the cowardice that dares not
    face the truth,
From that big bag of "fun size"
    Baby Ruths,
From the urgings of my unrelenting
    sweet tooth,
I pray, dear Lord, deliver me.

Lead me not into snacking, nor the
    Häagen-Dazs store,
And to disdain the beef jerky I so adore,
Let me not eat a hot dog and crave
    "just one more,"
From temptations of junk food,
    deliver me!

PLEA TO SAINT ANTHONY

Like prodigal children, they've strayed
    from the fold
Those umbrellas and ballpoints I've owned.

And so many times I've got only one sock
While its mate's in a venue unknown.

O when will my precious coat buttons
    come back?
O when will those stubborn things learn?

I'll welcome them home! I'll forgive
    and forget—
If thou makest my lost things return.

INTERCESSION FOR THOSE WHO MEANT WELL

God who gives us all good things,
Guide my friends toward
A more imaginative array of presents
On your Son's birthday this year.
Please forsake all Clappers,
SaladShooters,
Popeil's Pocket Fishermen,
Ugly Neckties,
Chia Pets,
Signature Fragrances Based on TV Characters,
And indeed anything whose name
    begins with "Amazing"
And ends with "O-matic."
Amen.

BEVERAGE
BENEDICTION

Benevolent Master,
Be merciful and let this Coke machine
Accept my crumpled dollar bill.
Yea, verily, it is wrinkled
And the corner is torn,
But I have a great thirst
And no change.*

*Ecclesiastes also mentioned vending machines:
"O Lord, let me not put in my money and then see the
'Make Another Selection' light."

PETITION
OF THE
SLOTHFUL

Lord,
You transformed water into wine,
Lot's wife into a pillar of salt,
And parted the Red Sea.
So as I sit on my couch
Without my remote control
Wilt thou change MTV
Back to ESPN.*

*Some biblical scholars contend that this appeal will work
only for someone wanting to change to a religious channel.
However, the theory remains unproved because no one has
ever actually wanted to do this.

THE FINAL
SEND-OFF

Into thy hands
I commend my broken
      answering machine,
The air conditioner that blows
      warm air,
The CD player that skips,
The microwave that won't open,
The steam iron that leaks brown water.

They served me a short time on Earth,
But now cause me only great grief.
So I ask of you, Lord,
Remind me next time to send in
      the warranty cards.

PRE-PLUNGE PRAYER

O Mighty One,
I have endured the log flume
With its steep drop into chilly waters,
And countless other thrill rides
At the behest of my foolhardy
     companions.
Now, as this Viper roller coaster
Takes me to the top of its mile-high
     peak,
I beg you:
Before we get to the upside-down loops
And 65-mph speeds,
Pray let me not perish
Because of a loose screw somewhere,
And if thou chooseth that I not lose
     my life today,
Let me also not lose my lunch.

TRAVELS
AND
TRIBULATIONS

~

Lord, I thank thee for guiding
my flight
Safely to Chicago:
Now, please
help my luggage do the same.

~

HIGHWAY MEDITATION

O let those flashing lights I see
In my rearview mirror
Be after the guy in front of me
Driving the Cavalier.

But if it's me the trooper seeks
And he pulls me off the road,
May he heed my sobs and shrieks
And tickets not bestow.

Yet if a ticket I receive
And into court I go,
Make sure that the judge believes
    my lies
And let the cop not show!

PRAYER FOR
ROOM
AT THE INN

O Lord, as I reach my journey's end,
Please ensure that this hotel has a record
    of my reservation
For the nonsmoking double I specifically
    requested.
Guide the bellhop swiftly to my room.
Keep him from demonstrating
How to operate the bathroom light
    and the curtains
In a shameless attempt to get a tip.
Steady the air conditioner,
That it may not rumble like a freight train.
Grant that there be a functioning ice machine
    on this floor
And that the television receives more
    than three channels.
And as I remember thee in my prayers each night,
Let them remember my wake-up call
    in the morning.

AN INNOCENT ABROAD

Dear God,
You have created many magical lands
In this most wondrous of worlds.
So during my trip abroad,
Allow me to enjoy that which you have
     created
Without the distraction of any armed
     insurgencies.
Yea, when I dine on one of the
     "local specialties,"
Let me not choose the marinated toad's meat
Or shredded lamb's hoof in spider sauce.
But if I do,
Help me to swiftly discern the difference
Between the door to the men's and
     the ladies' rooms.
Amen.

SOUTH OF THE BORDER SUPPLICATION*

O Heavenly Father,
I have drunk from the Unholy Water,
So as I sit upon this earthly throne,
Hear my vacation prayer:
Please let me see more of Cancún
Than just the inside
Of this bathroom stall.

*See also: Leviticus's exultation:
"Praise be to thee, Pepto-Bismol!"

PRAYER
BEFORE
TAKEOFF

The multitudes are surging forward
Like the heathen fleeing Gomorrah.
Surely they cannot all be flying first class or
    traveling with small children.
Grant patience, Lord, patience to them.

They are hoisting their too-big bags to
    the overhead compartments,
Some far too large to ever fit in.
They have crushed my neatly folded jacket in
    their haste—
Grant peace, Lord, peace to them.

And now the big, sweaty man in the cowboy hat
Is heading down the aisle, looking
    toward my row.
He is eyeing seat 6B, right next to mine—
Grant seat 7B, Lord, seat 7B to him.

IN-FLIGHT MEDITATION

Thou who soareth with angels,
Pray bring me comfort on this four-hour
   flight.
Shield me from the turbulence that starts as
   soon as the meal is served.
Prevent those sitting in front of me from
   reclining their seats into my tiny space.

Silence the snoring businessman,
   as well as the kid's video game.
And, Lord, when I rush into the aisle,
   in dire need of the restroom,
Let them not be there with that damned
   beverage cart
Blocking the way.*

*See also: Matthew's reference to airline food:
 "What foul thing hast thou unleashed from the galley onto
 my tray table, O Lord?"

THE LEGACY
OF BABEL

O Master of Many Tongues,
Tear the cobwebs away from my aging brain.
Enlighten me so I am able
To conjugate the verb "to be"
In this beautiful but incomprehensible
    language.
Give me the power to make these vowel
    sounds,
The "ä" and "é" and "ieu,"
And to boldly roll my R's like a pro.
O help me understand why every noun has
    a gender,
Why a door is more feminine than masculine.
My trip abroad is three weeks from now
And I would like to communicate with
    the natives,
Not just smile and point.

NOVENA FOR THE FAMILY VACATION

Precious Lord, take my hand—
Get me out of this minivan.

I thought the turn was at Exit Four,
But now we're lost on a wild detour.

I am tired. I am worn.
The map is long since ripped and torn.

Guide me with thy precious light,
To a decent place we can spend
    the night.*

*If your path leads you to a Motel 6, your entire family
should pray intensely for several additional hours.

MEDITATION
ON A
TAXI RIDE

O make this cabbie hear my plea
And get me where I need to be.

Please let him watch the road with zeal
And keep both hands upon the wheel.

Pray silence his unceasing talk
On this our third trip round the block.

O Lord, if you can't ease my strain
Perhaps next time I'll take the train.

THE LAST MILE*

Heavenly Father,
As my gas-gauge needle
Hovers ever so close to the "E,"
Please let a few precious gas fumes
And my faith in thy power
Be enough to get my thirsty Toyota
To the next Exxon station.

For more on spontaneous automotive healing, see page 51.

LIFE'S LITTLE TRIALS

~

Please let them realize, Lord,
That locating the smoking section
Right next to the nonsmoking section
Is contrary to thy laws of physics.

~

THE NEW TEN COMMANDMENTS

1. Thou shalt not keep talking on a pay phone when others are clearly waiting to use it.

2. Thou shalt not walk when the sign says "Don't Walk."

3. Honor thy friends by not subjecting them to six pictures of your new baby.

4. Thou shalt not enter the "10 Items or Less" line with a full shopping cart.

5. Thou shalt not drink all the milk and put the empty carton back in the fridge.

6. Honor thy Webmaster and thy personal trainer.

7. Thou shalt not play thy Walkman so loud that people twenty feet away can sing along.

8. Thou shalt let the exiting passengers off the elevator before attempting to get on.

9. Thou shalt have thy money ready before pulling up to the toll booth.

10. Thou shalt always, ALWAYS signal before making a left-hand turn.

GROCERY GRACE

Lord, there's really nothing super
About this line at the supermarket.
Wilt thou prevent the multitudes
    in front of me
From paying by check?
Can thou keep them from questioning
    the price of the asparagus
And getting into long conversations
    with the clerk?
Wilt thou forestall them from attempting
    to redeem expired coupons
And insisting upon digging for exact change
In the deep recesses of their pocketbooks?
Only thou hast the power, Lord,
To ensure that their items pass successfully
    through the scanner,
So that we don't have to wait for
    price check
All the way from Aisle 9.

PLEA TO SILENCE PROUD PARENTS

I've listened with patience to all of the tales
Of their brilliant and talented kids:
How Caitlin's IQ measures right off the scales
And what great things their Jonathan did.

At baseball, the youngest's already a star
And the three-year-old plays violin.
Bernard's in third grade, but he's just
            passed the bar
While Anita can speak Mandarin.

O help moms and dads to their senses return
And recant the tall tales that they tell.
O Lord, let them cease all their bragging
            and learn
That it's *my* kids who really excel.

PARKING LOT HYMN

I thank thee, Lord, for guiding me
To a parking space that's free.
You let me beat that awful man
(With new Corvette and phony tan)
And sped me here in the nick of time,
To fit my car between the lines.
Oh praise to Mary, Paul and Peter—
There's still ten minutes on the meter.

IDES OF
APRIL

O Keeper of the
Heavenly Ledger,
Shield me from IRS examiners*
Who wouldst audit me this year,
Or any year for that matter.
Though I have been truthful in spirit,
In addition and subtraction
I may have sinned.

*Less politically correct readers may substitute
with "tax bandits."

ON REALLY NEEDING A COAT HANGER

Lord, I am already a half hour late.

Please let that glint of metal I just saw
As I locked my car door
Not be my keys
Dangling in the ignition.

1-800-
GOD-HELP*

Thou who knowest all things,
When I dial a number in need of help
And am commanded from on high to
    "Press one to proceed,"
Let me not get a recording saying
"Your call is important to us,"
Nor a long list of programmed options.

Instead let me be connected to another
    of those
Whom you created in your own image.
    Amen.

*This prayer should be invoked before attempting to
call your bank, your credit card company, the phone
company or any government agency.

SUPPLICATION FOR LITTLE FAILINGS

Great holder of keys to the wonders
of history,
Please let me unlock some of life's
little mysteries:

Just how do I program the new VCR
And open that "childproof" aspirin jar?
Pray tell me the difference between
"who" and "whom"
And how to get children to clean up
their rooms!

O Lord, I would feel that I'm not
such a dunce
If I managed to balance my checkbook—
just once!

PICNIC
BENEDICTION

Into every life
A little rain must fall.*

But please,
Just this once—
Not on the weekend.

*Noah's writings indicate that the Great Flood
was timed to begin with the first Saturday in summer,
to ensure that the maximum number of picnics
and barbecues would be rained out.*

RECYCLE THIS PRAYER

I want to do right by thy gracious
    natural gifts,
So stand at my side as I sift—
These bottles of brown and bottles
    of green,
Newsprint and jam jars and polystyrene,
White paper, soda cans—in a
    hodgepodge,
Blocking the hallway into the garage.

Help me to sort and to bundle
    and band,
For the Day of Recycling is nearly
    at hand!

LEISURELY PURSUITS

~

If I should die
before I wake,
Please tape *Seinfeld*.

~

SILENT FILM

Lord, strike these rude filmgoers mute
Them who insist on talking during
    the final reel:
Especially that woman who has to shout
Every last plot development to her husband;
And that man who feels the need
To address the main characters from his seat.
Quiet their crinkling candy wrappers
Before I give in to the urge to
    "Shhhhhhhush!"
(And finally, Lord, please grant acting lessons
    to Demi Moore.*)

*Readers are encouraged to pronounce Ms. Moore's first
 name the correct way, with the accent on the first syllable,
 lest God see fit to bestow us with Striptease 2.

DINING OUT
BLESSING

May the maître d' rise up to meet you
And not make you wait a half hour past
your reservation time.
May the waitress hear your plea for another
minute to decide
And then actually return in a minute, instead
of twenty.
May the chef interpret your order for a steak
cooked "medium"
To really and truly mean a steak cooked
with a little pink in the middle.
When the time finally comes to calculate
15% of $53.21—
May God help you.

POP CULTURE CONFESSION

O Lord, I must confess
I don't watch PBS
And neither do I view
McLaughlin and his crew.

I wish I were the kind
Who really tried to find
The high-quality TV
You'd like for me to see.

But every day I turn
The dial to Howard Stern
Or *Baywatch* or a show
Like *90210*.

O Lord, please help me to erase
My love for *Melrose Place*.

SPORTS WIDOW'S LAMENT

I have known the mornings, evenings,
    afternoons
Here on my own while he is
    wandering free.
I've heard his tales of runs and extra points
And long endured the matches on TV.

Next Sunday, if you cannot change his mind
And once again I'm left without his help,
Then please send down a storm
    to wash the car
And kindly teach the lawn to mow itself.

BEFORE THE DINNER PARTY

Hold this soufflé firm, O Lord,
Yea let it stand proud and tall.
I know you won't let me run out of ice
Nor allow the spiced rum cake to fall.

Under thy calm and watchful eye,
I'm sure all will go smoothly tonight.
You will not let me burn the rice
And will keep these new candles alight.

With you on my side, I'll remember the
    names
Of Beth's husband and Gregory's wife,
And the evening will be something special
    and nice—
Not the longest four hours of my life.

PSALM OF THE WEEKEND GARDENER

Deliver thy nature's bounty to me, Lord:
Keep my tomatoes safe from aphids
And protect their roots from fungus.
Shield my little roses,
Which I have babied all spring long
From that last blast of chilling frost.
Let the sun shine warm on
    my red leaf lettuce
And wither the weeds that grow
    among my azaleas.
Lead the deer and the rabbits to
    some other backyard,
And bring forth abundance
    on my little plot.

AEROBICS PLEA

Let thy vengeance fall, O Lord,
Upon this aerobics instructor,
She who has thighs like iron
And a capacity for torture that
    seems endless.
Let her not shout
    "OK, twenty more lunges!"
In that perky soprano
As my knees buckle.

When I emerge from class,
Drenched and disheveled,
Let that not be the moment
I finally run into
    That cute guy with the Lexus.

GOLFER'S GRACE

The Lord is my shepherd, who guideth
    my golf ball
And maketh it lie down in
    His green fairways.
He leadeth it beside (but not into)
    the still waters,
And bringeth it safely to rest near the pin.
Yea, though I walk through
    the sand traps and rough,
The Lord steereth me, with hopes
    of a birdie to save this round.
And if not, I will take comfort
When my cup runneth over
    (in the clubhouse later on).

WWW. GOD-BE PRAISED.COM

Internet problems are plaguing me,
Lord of the Information
    Superhighway—
Outdated Web pages and busy signals
Vex me every time I try to connect.
Eliminate all the on-line infidels,
Chasten those "spammers" who send
    me junk e-mail,
Investment scams and pyramid schemes,
Not to mention temptations of
    "89,000 Internet Addresses."
Deliver me from Cyberspace,
    Holy Webmaster,
Ye who have the most exalted of
    High-Speed Access!

A FINAL PRAYER

All I ask of thee is to
Grant me the good taste,
Thoughtfulness,
And, if necessary,
The seven bucks
To purchase the sequel
To this wonderful book.

~